Caring All Around Me
WORKBOOK
Coloring & Exercises for Healthy Relating

written and illustrated by
TIA RICHARDSON

For more of Tia's work, please visit
www.cosmic-butterfly.com

In a world of suffering
Trouble and Fear
In my Heart there's a doorway
drawing me near

A Garden of Possibilities
Might show the Way
To a brighter World
One sunny day

Every thought we think, every dream we imagine
Brave enough to share
Goes out into the World on Rays of Light
Brave enough to care

THIS WORKBOOK IS DEDICATED TO ALL WHO ARE STRUGGLING TO AWAKEN

A GUIDE FOR READERS

The stories, activities, and ideas shared in this workbook are based on the book *Caring All Around Me*, written and illustrated by Tia Richardson.

In this workbook, young people can create their own journey using a template as a guide for their own discovery about healthy relating — to themselves and to life. Helpful suggestions are provided for how these exercises can be used in everyday life.

Some exercises use fill in the blanks, and others use coloring and drawing. No art skills are necessary to join the fun! Markers, crayons, and colored pencils may be used. This workbook can be adapted for individuals or groups.

ADDITIONAL RESOURCES FOR PARENTS & TEACHERS

At the end of this workbook, more insight is offered into ways to expand upon what is included here. A mini journal offers space for more reflection. Also included are a list of definitions, reflection questions, and a bonus activity that can be done outside of the workbook.

AUDIO GUIDES

Audio guides for certain activities, including the meditation, can be found at the artist's website: www.cosmic-butterfly.com.

HOPE

Fill in the SUN'S RAYS with your own CARING WORDS

One day when I was _____,
the bright sun shone warmly on my skin. Floating on the buttery rays of light,
I saw all kinds of messages! Some were caring, but some were not.

Caring all Around Me: Workbook | cosmic-butterfly.com

Write caring messages for the flowers in the rays of light.

Caring all Around Me: Workbook I cosmic-butterfly.com

"Everything in the world thrives on a positive flow of *light, life, and love.* You can't see it, but you can feel it."

A **ROSE** struggled to grow in a dark place. There was a **BIG ROCK** blocking a ray of sunlight, almost crushing her. A **MESSAGE OF HOPE** tried to get through but couldn't.

We all need some basic things to help our bodies survive, like food, clothing, water and shelter. There are other basic things everybody needs to help our minds and feelings be healthy, too. When we don't have these it can cause stressful feelings. Think of yourself as the rose. Think of the rock as a challenge in your life.

WE ALL NEED TO BELONG, TO FEEL JOY, TO BE SAFE, AND TO FEEL CARED ABOUT.

A VOICE IN THE HEART

Our INNER VOICE can GUIDE us in LIFE.

"Everything in the world thrives on a flow of light, life, and love. You can't see it, but you can feel it. The messages are all around us, and there are caring messages for everyone. Sometimes things don't go as planned, and the flow gets blocked. When this happens, it causes suffering."

IN A WORLD OF SUFFERING TROUBLE AND FEAR IN MY HEART THERE'S A DOORWAY DRAWING ME NEAR

In the book, Mara describes some challenges and feelings of suffering after the loss of a friend, failing a test, and regretting her choices.

Mara found a voice inside her heart giving her helpful guidance: *"Even when suffering happens, we have to look for the messages that remind us we are still valuable"*.

This means that when a challenge happens, you can think of a choice you or others can make that you believe will help make it better. The best part is, there are lots of ways something can be made better! To do this, we need to have an open mind. Then we can think creatively and use our imagination!

In this section, we will use the power of our creative imagination to think about ways to help challenges get better. When it comes to our imagination, the sky is the limit! Try these exercises out for yourself, and find if that is **true for you!**

CHOICES

In this exercise, think of a challenge you have experienced and write a sentence sharing what happened. Then, think of a choice you believe you or others can make that will help make it better.

Example:
Even when my best friend doesn't like me anymore,
I can still care about others and know my good friends accept me for who I am.

Even when _____
_____,
I can still _____
_____.

Even when _____
_____,
I can still _____
_____.

Keys for Adults

The idea here is to try to put the situation, no matter how big or small, into a simple sentence. The first step to healing is offering a person a chance to freely acknowledge what the challenge is. The second step is thinking of a choice that they or others can make to help make it better. The third step is imagining a future as a result of those choices.

The key to the 'I can still' exercise is defining a choice the person can make that they believe will help make their challenge better. The choice can be real or imaginary! No matter how big or small or out of reach it may seem, the person needs to be free to express what they think will help.

Caring all Around Me: Workbook I cosmic-butterfly.com

MAZE of CHALLENGES

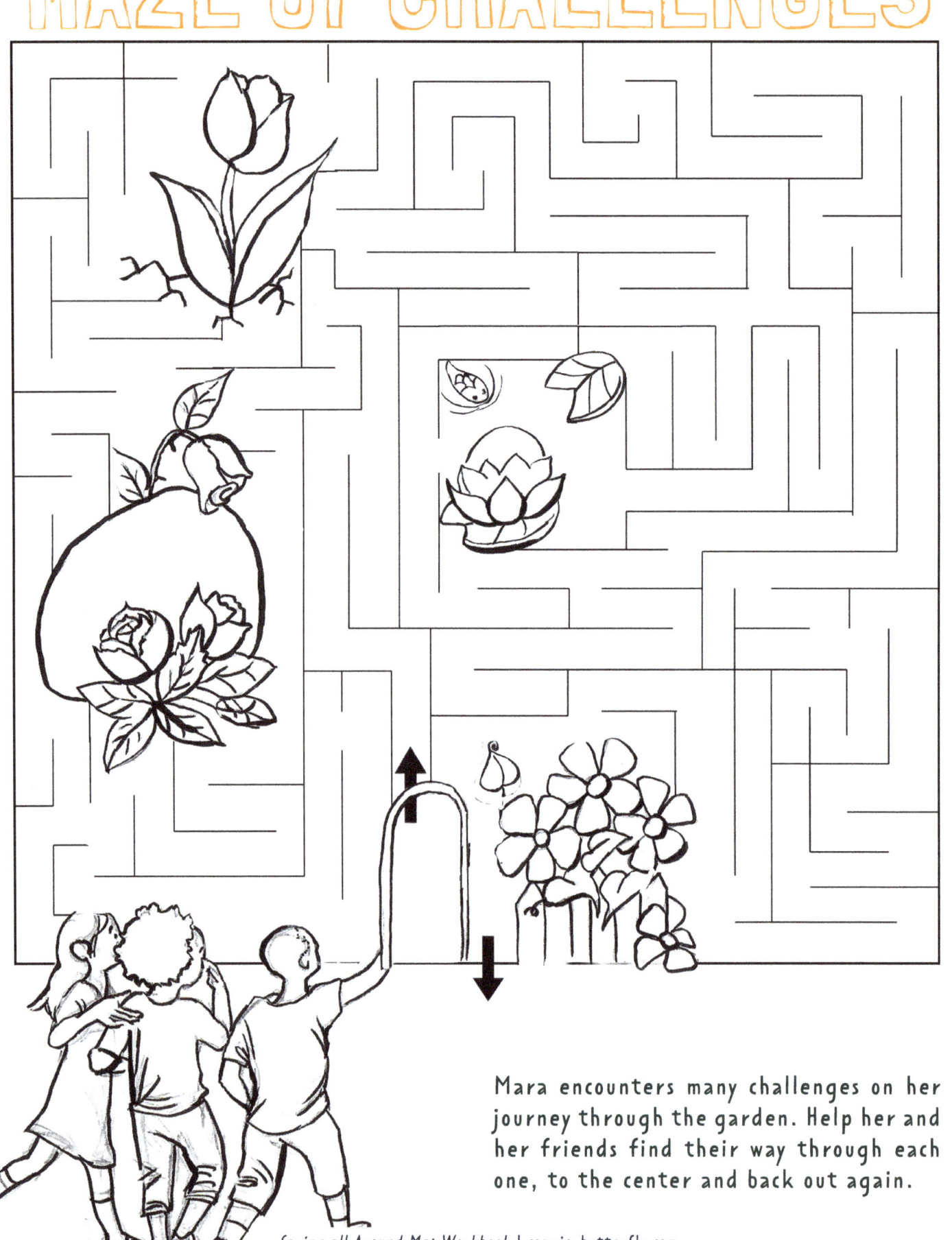

Mara encounters many challenges on her journey through the garden. Help her and her friends find their way through each one, to the center and back out again.

Caring all Around Me: Workbook | cosmic-butterfly.com

But something was wrong

In another part of the garden, things looked very different.

Those flowers weren't getting *any* messages.

Think of yourself as one of the roses trying to grow. Think of the rock as a challenge in your life. What's one thing that is difficult or challenging for you in your life? It could be in school, home, family, or something else. Maybe it's something you feel or think about yourself.

Draw a picture of the challenge blocking the rose from growing. Then, write a caring message trying to get to it.

Finish the sentence:
Something was wrong. I noticed one unhappy rose struggling to grow in a place that was too dark and unsafe.

There was a _____

_____ blocking a ray of sunlight.

Caring all Around Me: Workbook | cosmic-butterfly.com

Think of a choice you can make to help the challenge you just drew get better for the rose. What's one thing you can do?

Finish the sentence:
I decided to help the rose get the caring message by _____
_____.

Draw a picture that shows how you can help the rose get the caring message.

A SAFE PLACE

Definition: a place that helps a person feel like they are free to be themselves, relax, and feel cared for.

ABUNDANCE

UNDERSTANDING

RESPECT

In the book, Mara finds a community garden where she feels safe with all of the caring messages around her.

"Sometimes people need space to understand each other just like the vines. When I need space, I go to a favorite place. Sometimes I sit and think, or write, or daydream. When I do that, it makes me feel better. With all of the caring messages streaming in, this garden is a perfect spot!"

FEELING SAFE

We can feel safe when we are calm, relaxed, free, and happy. There are lots of healthy ways to have these feelings. This is an exercise you can do on your own or talk about with someone you trust. You may even discover a new way for yourself!

Examples of feeling safe:

- I feel safe when I feel like someone is listening to me.
- I feel safe when someone I know sticks up for me when I'm being bullied.
- I feel safe when somebody helps me when I ask.

Finish the sentence with one thing you or someone else can do to help you feel safe. Then, draw a picture of it.

I feel safe when _____

_____

DRAW YOUR SAFE PLACE

What is a place that helps you feel safe? It can be real or imaginary. Now, imagine yourself in that place. Look up, down, and all around you. What do you see, hear, taste, touch, and smell? Write about a place where you can do what helps you feel safe.

One place I can do that is _____

_____

SELF-CARE

Definition: a healthy activity we can do to care for our body, mind, or spirit that helps us feel better.

Just like trimming and weeding the vines, what we do to care for ourselves can help us feel better. In the book, Mara names what she does for self-care in the garden because she feels safe there with all of the caring messages around her. Writing in a journal, playing, riding a bike, dancing, drawing, and listening to music are some things that help her.

What are some things you can do for self-care?

_____

_____

_____

_____

Caring all Around Me: Workbook | cosmic-butterfly.com

**Draw yourself in the picture above.
Draw one thing you can do for self care in each box below.**

THE LOTUS FLOWER

I am a lotus flower. I have roots that grow in thick river mud.

Every night, I close and sink under the river water to sleep where it is safe, because my thick, waxy petals keep the mud from sticking.

Every morning, the rising sun wakes me from my sleep. Then I rise above the water and open each petal just as beautiful as the day before.

We can be like the lotus when stressful things happen, by going to our safe place and rising again with each new day.

RESILIENCE: being able to adapt to or recover from challenging situations.

MANTRA: Every day begins in a new way. Today I am anew.

CREATE YOUR OWN FLOWER POEM

Look up a type of flower you like. Learn about what their roots and petals need to grow strong and healthy. Why are they able to adapt or recover from challenges in their environment? Can you think of different ways you might be like this flower – at night, and also in the morning?

I am a _____.

I have roots that grow in _____.

Every night I _____.

because _____.

Every morning I _____.

because _____.

GRATITUDE
Opening Each Petal One By One...

Think of a situation that you feel stressed about. Next to each root, write something about that situation that bothers you. On each petal, write one thing you can appreciate in the present moment. It may or may not be related to the situation. When we feel stress, finding something we can appreciate in the moment can be uplifting.

MEDITATION

Definition: an exercise to help the body and mind feel calm and focused through breathing, guided reflection, and other techniques.

Many people from different cultures around the world have practiced meditation for thousands of years to help them feel calm, less stressed, and even to discover new things about themselves! There are lots of ways to meditate, and there is no right or wrong way. The key is to do what feels right for you!

How do you begin to know what feels right for you? One way is to try it for yourself and notice what you feel!

BASIC MEDITATION GUIDELINES

1. Begin by finding a quiet place. It's better when there are no distractions around like noise, people talking, or electronic devices on. Any place can be a good place to meditate where you can feel safe, comfortable, and relaxed.

2. Use a pillow, blanket, or cushion to sit on in a comfortable position that you can hold for a few minutes, such as cross-legged or seated in a chair.

3. Choose to sit quietly or meditate with music. Quiet music may be played during meditation that is designed to help calm the body's nervous system and help the mind focus on the present moment. There are many styles of music that do this naturally. Gentle instrumental music, soft music without lyrics, and the new age genre are a few examples. You can also use an instrument like a chime or singing bowl at the beginning to bring you a sense of harmony.

4. Prepare your body to feel calm by taking a few slow, deep breaths. Inhale deep into your belly. Then exhale, imagining your thoughts and feelings flowing down a big golden ray of light through your body and into your feet, into the earth.

5. Set a time limit. You can follow along with a guided meditation or sit quietly in silence for a few minutes. The next exercise lasts about five minutes.

6. You can meditate alone or in a group. If in a group, it is better if everyone does the same meditation, so there is less distraction.

7. The meditation on the next page can be read by another person or read and prerecorded and played back. It is also available by the author as an audio recording on the website www.cosmic-butterfly.com.

MEDITATION FOR INNER LIGHT

CARRY YOUR OWN FLOW OF light, life, and love WHEREVER YOU GO!

Imagine a sparkling pond in the middle of a grassy field on a bright, sunny day.

Along the edge of the pond are bright, colorful flowers. Imagine yourself sitting next to the pond. Feel the warm breeze as it brushes across your skin. A ray of golden sunlight shines down brightly over the pond. The golden ray makes a bright reflection in the shape of a ball of white light in the middle of the pond. See it round and brightly lit, almost like an electric mist.

Slowly, this ball of light begins to lift off the water and float right above the surface. It stretches out to everything around it. As it reaches towards you, you step into this bright light. Let yourself sit in this ball of light for a moment. Notice how it feels. It could feel peaceful, quiet, and welcoming. It embraces you.

Now just in front of your eyes, a flower bud begins to appear. It slowly opens, and the center glows brightly with a caring respect. See this healing energy flow into the environment, freely sharing its energy with everything around.

Now come back into your body and feel the ground beneath you again. Slowly come back to where you are and open your eyes.

Caring all Around Me: Workbook | cosmic-butterfly.com

FINDING COMMUNITY

In the book, Tulip felt **ISOLATED** and **ALONE**, like he didn't belong. All living beings need to **BELONG** and feel **CARED ABOUT**.

A COMMUNITY OF TULIPS

Finish the sentence. Then, pick one to draw in the box.

One thing I can do to care for myself is _____

_____.

I feel cared for when others _____

_____

One thing that helps us feel like we belong and are cared about is helping and supporting each other. When we volunteer or do acts of kindness with an attitude of helping others, no matter how big or small, it can help us feel better about ourselves, because we are participating as part of something bigger than ourselves.

Another thing that helps people feel like part of a community is doing activities together with friends, our families, or community groups.

MARA HELPED THE TULIP BY MOVING HIM TO A SUNNY SPOT IN THE GARDEN

Connect the dots to find what message he gave her.

FRIENDSHIP

SELF-ACCEPTANCE: being able to appreciate and understand your own strengths and weaknesses.

Even when suffering happens, we have to look for the messages that remind us we are still valuable.

Even when we don't feel accepted by others, we can still accept ourselves by having the courage to look and see what we can appreciate or like about ourselves. You might be surprised what you discover if you give yourself a chance!

Use the space below to list: Who makes you feel accepted? What's one thing they appreciate about you? What's one thing you appreciate about yourself? About someone else? Examples: Caring, Generous, Honest, Smart, Creative.

WE ALL CAN WIN!

Flowers at the bottom of a tall fence are getting trampled in a rush to reach the light. Help them find their way, so they can be free!

GARDEN LABYRINTH

Help Mara and her friends walk the labyrinth to the calm, sparkling pond in the center of the garden. Fun fact: Labyrinths are often used by people to help themselves focus, feel calm, and notice what there is to appreciate in the moment.

CARING MAKES THE WORLD A BETTER PLACE

The voice in my heart spoke gently, "Those uncaring messages were thought of or spoken by other people in the world. If we don't let them in they go back into the soil as compost. Working with the earth, our friends underground happily munch and chop and chew until the uncaring messages become messages of love."

EVERY THOUGHT
WE THINK
AND EVERY DREAM
WE IMAGINE
BRAVE ENOUGH TO SHARE
GOES OUT INTO THE WORLD
ON RAYS OF LIGHT
BRAVE ENOUGH TO CARE

CARING ATTITUDES

ATTITUDE: A way of thinking, acting, or believing about something.

COMMON CARING ATTITUDES:

CARING	ACCEPTANCE	RESPECT	COURAGE	APPRECIATION
FRIENDLY	YOU CAN DO IT	SHARING	OPEN-MINDED	JOY

Even when we come across an uncaring message, we can still choose to turn it into caring energy again through our attitude.

DEFINITONS

Appreciation	Feeling thankful for something about oneself, others, or a situation.
Acceptance	Being able to understand or appreciate strengths and weaknesses about oneself, others, or a situation.
Caring	feeling or showing acceptance, appreciation, and respect to oneself or others
Courage	Being able to face a challenge even while feeling fear.
Joy	Feeling happy or a sense of well-being.
Open-mind	Being open to the possibilities in oneself, others, or a situation without judgement

Tip: Try on a caring attitude to see how it feels. The more you try, the better you get at it! With practice, it gets easier to use with uncaring messages. You might be surprised at what you can discover about yourself through the power of your attitude!

Turn uncaring messages into CARING ENERGY

41

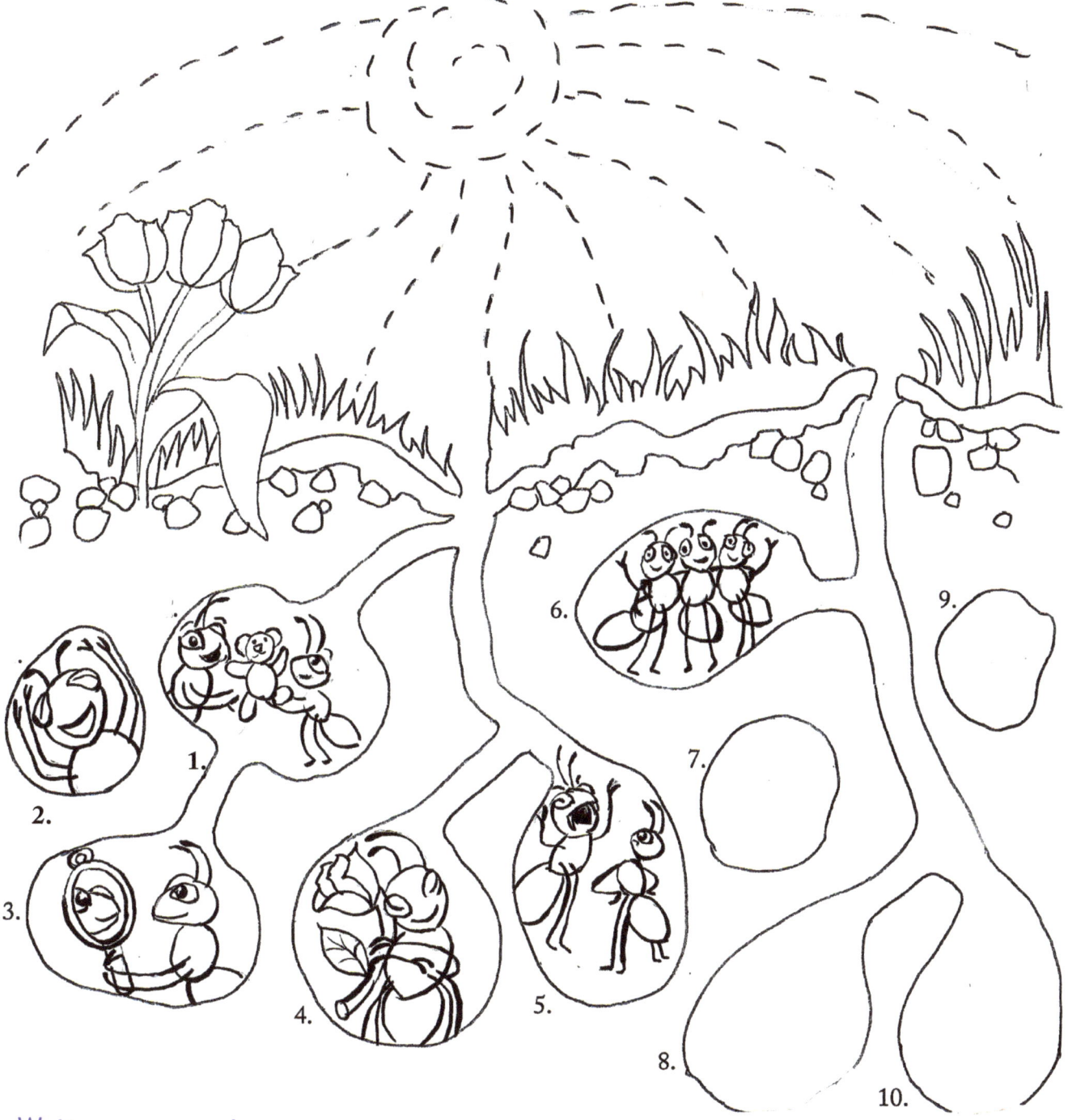

1. Write an uncaring message on each ray of the sun.
2. Look at the picture of ants. Find a caring attitude from the list that matches the picture. #1 is done for you.
3. Write a caring attitude on lines two through six that matches the numbers of the pictures. **4:** Create your own caring attitudes or use the list to finish numbers seven through ten.

1. _sharing_   6. _____
2. _____   7. _____
3. _____   8. _____
4. _____   9. _____
5. _____   10. _____

Caring all Around Me: Workbook | cosmic-butterfly.com

THOUGHTS ARE THINGS

"Do you know what happens to every thought we think and every dream we imagine? They go out into the world on **rays of light.**"

CARING BASKET OF LIGHT

What message would you put in your basket of light to help others in the world feel cared about? Draw a picture of it.

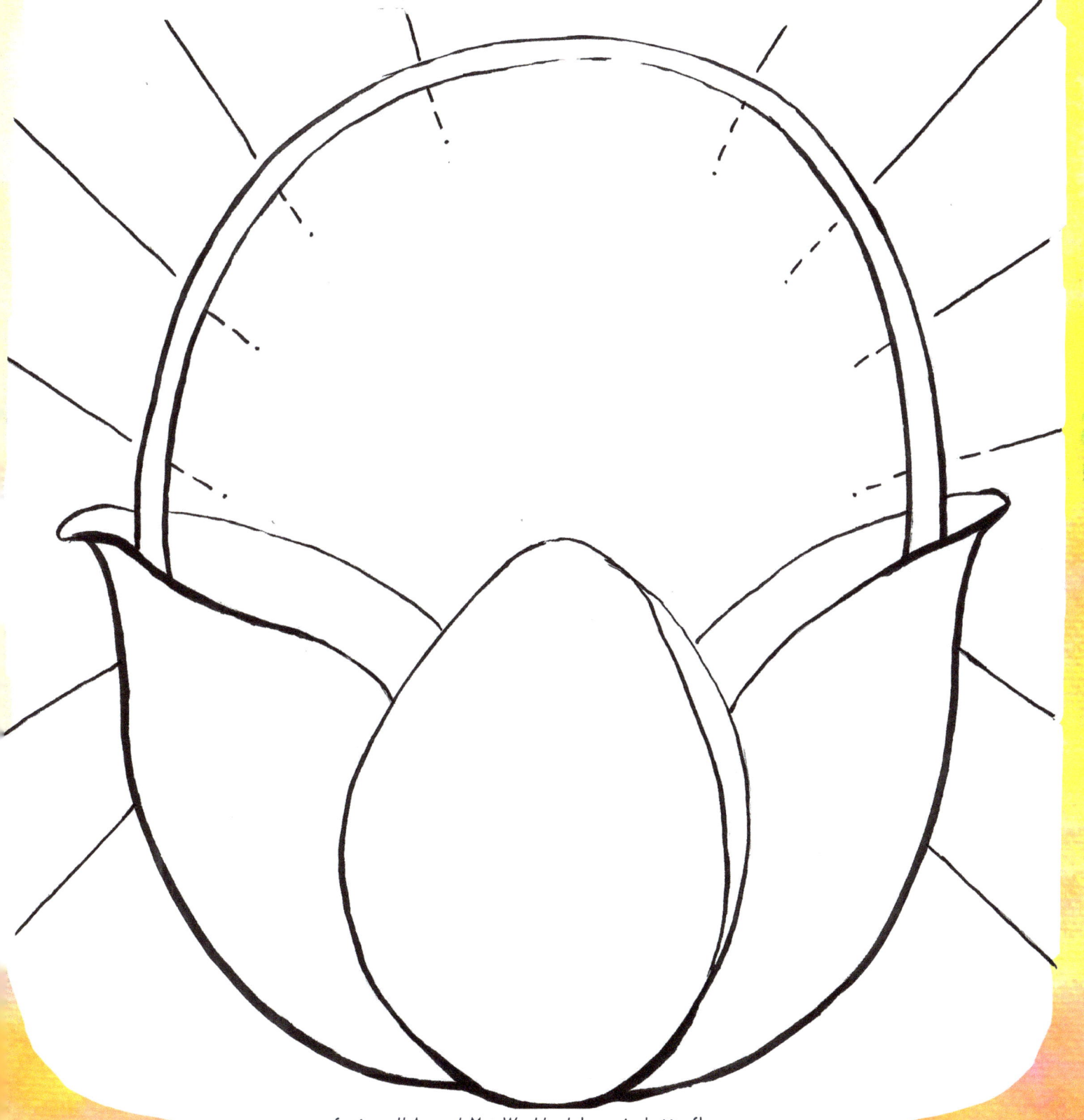

Caring all Around Me: Workbook | cosmic-butterfly.com

"The light carries little fairies who hold tiny baskets of light-filled messages. Their job is to deliver every message to all the world. Other living things help spread them, like your new butterfly friend."

"Sharing what's on our **HEARTS** helps others **CARE**."

As if on cue, one shy, beautiful lotus in the middle of the pond slowly opened each petal one by one.

'I want to be like the flowers and **SHARE** the caring I feel inside to **HELP OTHERS.**

Caring all Around Me: Workbook | cosmic-butterfly.com

IF YOU COULD BE A FLOWER WHAT KIND WOULD YOU BE?

If I were a flower, I would be a _____

because _____

I would be the colors _____

because _____

The love in Mara's heart taught her that she can send a caring message into the world to share with others. What would your message be?

The message I want to send is: _____

_____

Draw and color it here.

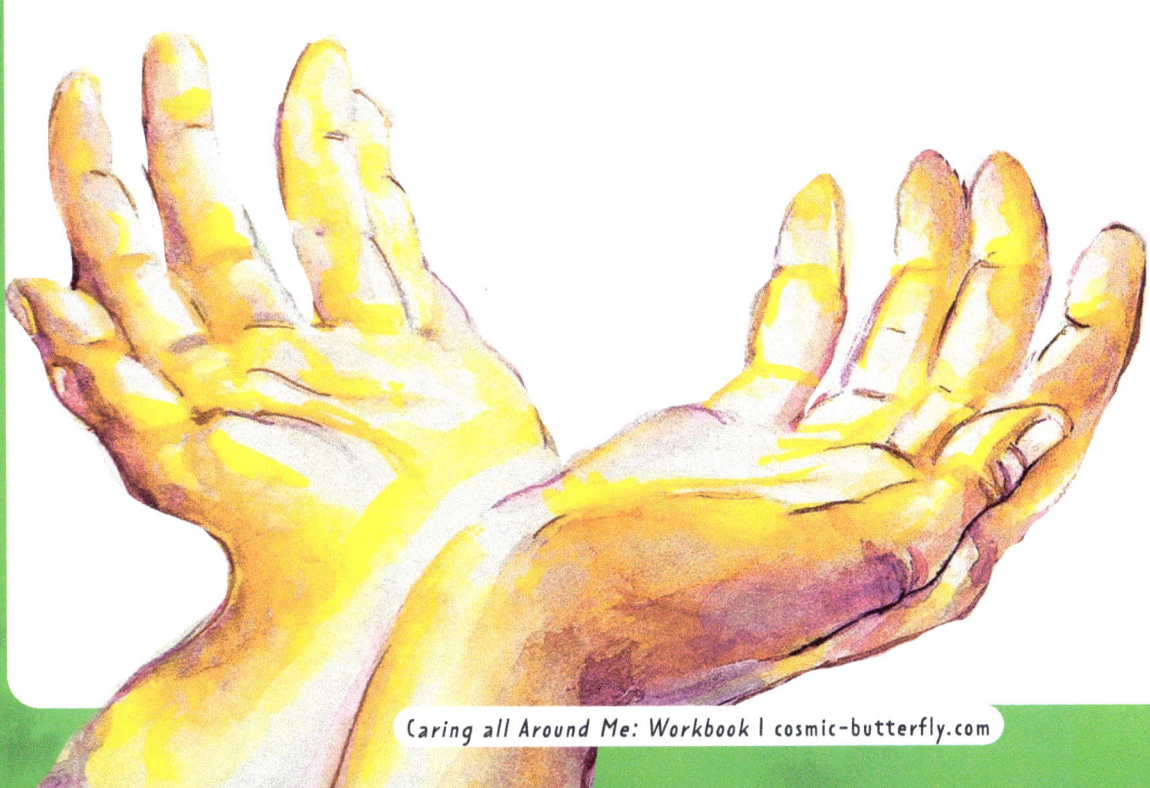

THINGS I APPRECIATE ABOUT MYSELF

THINGS I DISCOVERED ABOUT MYSELF

THERAPEUTIC WATERCOLORS EXERCISE

This exercise is a free form expression for self-discovery. The reflection questions are asked after completing the exercise. (Recommended for kids and adults, ages seven and up.)

Set-up:
Place the watercolors, brush, and paper on a table. The primary colors have a powerful effect on the human psyche. Many popular logos and symbols in advertising and art (Ex. Superman logo, Piet Mondrian) have used them. The goal of this exercise is to notice: what do you feel?

Demo (five minutes):
Look at the watercolor in the example above as a demonstration. Notice how the colors interact with each other. Imagine each color as having its own personality.

Exercise (fifteen minutes):
Start the music. Feel free to play with the colors any way you like. Try to see if you can get the colors to interact in a way that feels harmonious to you. Remember, there is no right or wrong way to do this. It's more of a feeling than a thinking exercise! When you can feel a sense of harmony, the art is done! Turn off the music.

Reflection (ten minutes):
This can be done individually or one at a time in a group. Suggested reflection questions:
What's one thing you appreciate about your painting?
What did you feel while painting?
What's one thing that was challenging for you?
Were you able to find a sense of harmony in the colors?

What you'll need:
- Watercolors
- Watercolor/wet-media paper
- Brush
- Medium-size cup filled halfway with water
- Gentle music to calm the nervous system

- This activity can be adapted for groups. Reflection works best when everybody who wants to share has a minute or two to speak for each question.
- A group of ten usually completes all the steps in the activity within 40-45 minutes, making this ideal for smaller groups.
- Larger groups can do share-outs by asking only those who want to share, rather than going around to each person.

Visit
www.cosmic-butterfly.com for more!

POST-EXERCISE REFLECTION QUESTIONS

Asking questions intended for self-reflection can help a child develop mindful awareness of their feelings. This is a skill that, with time and practice, can develop the ability to process difficult emotions through thinking about one's feelings.

Having up to three questions can be useful after completing any of the activities in the book. It's better to let them come naturally as part of what the child seems to be experiencing. You may come up with your own to add to these!

What's one thing you appreciate about_____? (name a topic, word, etc.)
What did you feel while doing this exercise?
What did you notice while doing this exercise?
What's one thing that was challenging for you during this exercise?
Is there anything you would do differently next time?
What's one thing you discovered about yourself?

IDEAS FOR EXPANSION

Teachers, parents, caregivers, therapists, and others are free to use or adapt any of these activities for the classroom, for educational or therapeutic purposes. They can be adapted for group activities around socio-emotional themes and healthy relating.

Try broadening a child's understanding through:

group formats, discussing certain keywords or glossary terms, exploring what meaning or understanding the child already has of the exercise, topic, or word helping them think about how it might relate to a situation or experience in their life, journaling after each exercise in response to the reflection questions, being curious and open-minded about their inner process!

THERE IS A WHOLE INNER WORLD WAITING TO BE EXPLORED IN EACH INDIVIDUAL'S OWN UNIQUE WAY. THIS WORKBOOK IS INTENDED TO HELP YOU DISCOVER SOMETHING NEW ABOUT YOURSELF!

WORDS AND THEIR MEANING USED IN THE BOOK

ACCEPTANCE: being able to understand or appreciate strengths and weaknesses about oneself, others, or a situation.

APPRECIATION: feeling thankful for something about oneself, others, or a situation.

ATTITUDE: a way of thinking, acting, or believing about something.

CARING: feeling or showing acceptance, appreciation, and respect to oneself or others

COMMUNITY: a group of people sharing work, play. or life together.

COURAGE: being able to face a challenge even while feeling fear.

FRIENDSHIP: a bond of caring between people who like to spend time together

GRATITUDE: a feeling of appreciation.

INNER VOICE: the higher self or conscience of a person.

JOY: feeling happy or a sense of well-being.

MANTRA: a word or phrase repeated for calming or motivation.

MEDITATION: an exercise to help the body and mind feel calm and focused through breathing, guided reflection, and other techniques.

OPEN-MIND: Being open to the possibilities in oneself, others, or a situation without judgement

RESILIENCE: being able to adapt to or recover from challenging situations.

RESPECT: treating others how they want to be treated.

SAFE PLACE: a place that helps a person feel like they are free to be themselves, relax, and feel cared for.

SELF-ACCEPTANCE: being able to appreciate and understand your own strengths and weaknesses.

SELF-CARE: a healthy activity we can do to care for our body, mind or spirit that helps us feel better.

SHARING: giving what one has to another, and getting from another something they have.

THOUGHTS ARE THINGS: the idea that thoughts are energy that can produce results.

Published by Orange Hat Publishing 2022
ISBN 9781645385646

Copyrighted © 2022 by Tia Richardson
All Rights Reserved
Caring All Around Me: Workbook
Written & Illustrated by Tia Richardson

All rights reserved. This book or parts thereof may not be reproduced in any form, stored in any retrieval system, or transmitted in any form by any means—electronic, mechanical, photocopy, recording, or otherwise—without prior written permission of the publisher or author, except as provided by United States of America copyright law and fair use. For permission requests, write to the publisher at shannon@orangehatpublishing.com or to the author directly at tiachianti@gmail.com

www.orangehatpublishing.com

www.ingramcontent.com/pod-product-compliance
Lightning Source LLC
LaVergne TN
LVHW070949070426
835507LV00030B/3468